Questions to Bring You Closer to Mom

100+ Conversation Starters for Mothers and Children of Any Age

Stuart Gustafson and Robyn Freedman Spizman

adamsme
Avon, Massachuse

Published by Adams Media,
an F+W Publications Company
57 Littlefield Street
Avon, MA 02322
www.adamsmedia.com

ISBN 10: 1-59869-478-2
ISBN 13: 978-1-59869-478-9

Printed in the United States of America.

J I H G F E D C B A

Library of Congress Cataloging-in-Publication Data
is available from the publisher.

Harvey Mackay quote reprinted with permission from nationally syndicated columnist Harvey
Mackay, author of *New York Times* #1 bestseller *Swim with the Sharks Without Being Eaten
Alive.*

This publication is designed to provide accurate and authoritative information with regard to the
subject matter covered. It is sold with the understanding that the publisher is not engaged in
rendering legal, accounting, or other professional advice. If legal advice or other expert assistance is required, the services of a competent professional person should be sought.
    —From a *Declaration of Principles* jointly adopted by a Committee of the
American Bar Association and a Committee of Publishers and Associations

Many of the designations used by manufacturers and sellers to distinguish their products are
claimed as trademarks. Where those designations appear in this book and Adams Media was
aware of a trademark claim, the designations have been printed with initial capital letters.

This book is available at quantity discounts for bulk purchases.
For information, please call 1-800-289-0963.

From Stuart Gustafson—I wish to dedicate this book first to my fabulous coauthor Robyn Freedman Spizman, who has been such a strong supporter of this book and its predecessor from the first time she saw them. She has always been there when I had a question, and many times she had the answer for me even before I asked. I consider myself to be extremely fortunate to have her as a coauthor. And to my mom, about whom I thought a lot when writing this book. To my wife Darlene and our two children, Adrianne and Woodrow—thank you for your continual and unconditional support throughout this process.

From Robyn Freedman Spizman—I remain eternally grateful to Stuart Gustafson, for without his vision and extreme dedication to this book series, it would not have become a reality. To my parents Phyllis and Jack Freedman, who have shared with me the joy of the generations past and celebrated the goal of preserving the special memories we all hold near and dear to our hearts. And to my husband Willy and our children Justin and Ali, who make my life so worthwhile and create new memories that sustain me. And to Doug and Genie Freedman, Sam and Gena Spizman, Lois Blonder, and Ramona Freedman; and to my real-life angel Betty Storne and the Spizman Agency, Jenny Corsey, and my devoted and wonderful family and friends, too numerous to mention, you are permanently recorded in my mind and heart forever.

contents

acknowledgments

Once again we have been fortunate to have the support of the professional staff of Adams Media to guide us through the process of planning, writing, and editing. We want to particularly thank Karen Cooper, Director of Marketing; Beth Gissinger, Director of Publicity; Michael O'Brien, Senior Publicist; Paula Munier, Innovation Director; and Brendan O'Neill, Project Manager. We are also very privileged to have the professional expertise of a fantastic agent—we extend our thanks to Meredith Bernstein for her advice and assistance. And, finally, we wish to acknowledge the excellent work of Willy Spizman, Jenny Corsey, and the award-winning Spizman Agency for the help they have given us along with their many talents and publicity efforts promoting our books.

Foreword

Writing our first book, *Questions to Bring You Closer to Dad*, was such an emotional drain on me as I was drafting, rewriting, editing, re-editing, and then finally proofreading one more time. I shed a lot of tears during those many, many months of going from the book concept to the finished product, which contained so much more content and insight than I had originally envisioned.

Losing a loved one is always hard; having a parent's life needlessly taken is an even harder experience to accept. Writing that book turned out to be good therapy for me—albeit forty years later—and I know I now have a way to capture the memories of my dad from those who knew him best. While I certainly would prefer to have had him be alive as I was growing up and starting a family, I am now comfortable in knowing that the gathering of those memories is possible. And I now also have a way of capturing my own thoughts and memories so that I can pass them on to my children.

One of the benefits I gained from writing *Questions to Bring You Closer to Dad* was that it "gave me access" to my mom in a way that I did not have before. My mom is ninety years old and she lives six blocks from our house. But she keeps pretty much to herself (and her dog) because she does not want to interfere in our busy lives. Before the book, our conversations focused on current activities, or maybe a recent vacation she took with one of my brothers. We would not talk about her life as a child, or about her family—other than her sisters, whom I knew as Aunt Alma and Aunt Kay. She did not want to talk about any of that, just about how Dad was taken too early in life. (He was forty-eight when a drunk driver killed him and my grandfather.)

But as I was gathering content for *Questions to Bring You Closer to Dad*, I began asking Mom a few of the questions that are in that book. Asking her those questions allowed us to start having more open dialogue about our family, and about her family. We are slowly approaching the stage of being able to talk about everything, and thanks to my question asking and interest in her life, we have made amazing progress and I am very happy for that. My hope is that I will be able to sit down with her and step through the questions in this book so that I can learn more about her, which in turn tells me more about my heritage. I may fudge a bit and tell her that I am asking the questions to get information to pass on to her grandchildren—but she just might read through that angle of mine. Regardless of my approach, these precious memories are too important to not have written down.

That singular goal is the essence of this book—capture those precious memories today so that you will have no regrets tomorrow. We all take it for granted that our moms will be here and that we can always talk with them whenever we want. But life does not always go according to "our plan." The Latin saying *carpe diem* translates to "seize the day"—meaning to do what you can in the day that is here and now. Today is here, but tomorrow is never guaranteed.

When I teamed up with my prolific coauthor Robyn Spizman, who has written many books on expressing your feelings and sharing memorable moments, we set out to make sure that **Questions to Bring You Closer to Mom** would help anyone forge a closer bond with their mother. Robyn is extremely close with her mother, who is very communicative and loves to share her childhood stories and favorite memories. The questions in this book strengthened even their relationship by focusing on her mother's life and the times that meant the most to her. Robyn added, "Often, so much of the mother and daughter experience is focused on the daughter or daily routines and other people, but when you turn the tables and really focus on your mother and listen to her talk about her life, those special times she treasures and her reflections, you learn so many beautiful things that add significant meaning and enjoyment to the experiences you share. The questions in this book will act as jumpstarts to encourage conversation. Your interest in her will open the floodgate of moments in your mother's life that shaped her. You will also learn about your mother's life and the times that ultimately become a treasure trove of memories."

Whether you are a son or a daughter, the purpose of the questions in this book is to guide you on a heartfelt discovery that will provide a lifetime of insights, stories, and cherished thoughts to help you connect with the ones you love. This book will help you get started, but it's up to you to take the necessary steps. We wish you a meaningful and rewarding journey as you get closer to Mom.

Stuart Gustafson
Boise, Idaho

Part 1

How to Use This Book

How to Use This Book

A MOM WEARS SO MANY HATS IN LIFE. She's our encourager, philosopher, teacher, motivator, counselor, rule-maker, and, most often, our guiding light in life. We wish to congratulate you for taking an important step in life to honor her. By filling out the pages in this book, you are making an effort to let your mom know how much she means to you and how much you love her. In return, you'll also have a wealth of stories, insights, and lessons learned that reflect your mother's life and the legacy she wishes to have you carry on.

If you have the luxury of sitting down with your mother, you are a very fortunate person. Life has blessed you with the opportunity to get to know your mom in even more meaningful ways that will support and comfort you for years to come. Or perhaps you are a mom, and you have decided to fill out this book yourself and later present it to your children as a loving will of sorts—we think that's absolutely wonderful. Our goal is to make sure that every mom all over the world leaves not only memories of their heartfelt love, but also a legacy of loving thoughts—their ideas and beliefs expressed for generations to come.

If your mother is no longer alive, we hope to provide a special way to bring Mom's most special attributes and memories to light. With the help of the questions in this book, and through your family and other individuals who knew her, it is still possible to obtain the answers. All you have to do is make the time.

We begin with a section called "Types of Moms." This section details eighteen different types of moms. When you find the type that best describes your mom, you can refer to the accompanying ideas for ways to begin conversations with her. This section also suggests things you can do together, shows you how to have "Mom radar" for things she likes, and points out her pet peeves and how to avoid them.

We organized this book to assist you in documenting the details of your mother's life. Our goal is to help you provide a legacy that will forever serve as a written record. The pages following the "Types of Moms" section are divided into nine thematic sections. Each provides a thoughtful set of questions to ignite a conversation with your mom about the following topics:

- On Mom's Life
- On Our Family History
- On Mom's Values
- On Marriage and Relationships
- On Mom's Dreams and Goals
- On Parenting and Children

- On Mom's Legacy
- Who Knows Mom Best?
- Mom's Favorite Things

Before you begin, share with Mom each of these sections and the topics you'll be asking her about, and reassure her you will be getting to each topic. While it might be difficult, it's important not to interrupt her if she goes off on a tangent. If Mom enjoys rambling on, be prepared with knowledge of all the questions in this book and enter her stories or thoughts wherever they fit best.

To begin, start by asking one question and recording Mom's answer in this book. Conducting the questions as an interview is certainly more fun and can be written out and then transferred to this book, but if time or distance makes this impossible, there are certainly other options. You can record your conversations with Mom on tape or ask her to fill out some of the sections she might prefer to write for herself. You can also fill out her list of favorite things and then ask her for the answer, and see if your answers match. There are several ways you can go about gathering information if your mom is no longer living. We have these three suggestions:

1. The next time there is a family gathering—it can be as big as Thanksgiving dinner or as simple as a summer outing—

pull out this book. Tell your family that you want to get some information about Mom. Read a question, and then ask, "How would Mom have answered that?" You will likely hear several responses to any one question; there might even be a few differences in the answers. That's okay. Write them all down if you can.

2. **Write out some of the questions on your own paper, and send them out to family members and friends who knew your mom.** Provide some explanation about this new project you are working on. Tell them you have a lot of questions you are trying to answer as if your mom were answering them for you. Let these people know that there is no time deadline, but that you would appreciate their sending back anything they have within a month. As a courtesy, enclose a self-addressed, stamped envelope with your letter.

3. **Buy extra copies of this book**. Write up a cover letter telling everyone what you are doing. Then send two copies of the book along with your cover letter to family members and friends. Ask them to fill out as much as they can in one of the books and send it back to you. (Send them a pre-paid envelope to make it easier.) The other book is for them to keep—they can use it to develop their own keepsake of your mom, or they could use it to begin their own journey to find out more about their own moms.

We send our best wishes to you as you begin your quest to take a closer view and inside look at the woman you lovingly call "Mom."

"Types of Moms and Their Characteristics"

THERE'S A WORLD OF MOMS OUT THERE, and each one is different. While every mom is different, moms do fall into categories. Each type of mom has its own characteristics, and there are some key essentials about each type that can help you. The more that you know about these characteristics, and the more that you work to understand how they apply to your mom, the better understanding you will begin to have of your mom. You will also see how she communicates, and how you can communicate with her—not just a "How was your day?" talk, but a deeper communication that she holds within herself.

As you read through the categories, you will probably find that there are several categories that describe your mom. Generally, however, there is a single one that is central to her core—this is what truly defines her. This is what we call her central characteristic. It does not matter what the season of the year is; it does not matter if she is at work or on vacation; it does not matter if she is forty or if she is seventy—this basic core personality trait, or central characteristic, stays with her and best describes her, day in and day out.

There are, of course, secondary characteristics that come into play at different times. She may exhibit what appears to be a different central characteristic when she is hosting a party, for example, but that is actually just a secondary characteristic that has temporarily surfaced. Deep inside, her central characteristic has not changed; she has just allowed another one to be more dominant for a short time. When she goes on an action-packed vacation, a different secondary characteristic may surface.

The Benefits of Knowing Your Mom's Central Characteristic

- Knowing your mom's central characteristic will tell you a lot about her that you might not already know. This can also explain a lot about you—it is very likely that you have many of her tendencies. You might not want to admit certain pieces of it, but you are a lot like Mom. Now that you know this, you can see how other people see you and why they react to you the way that they do.
- You'll be able to talk to Mom about what interests her the most. Knowing her central characteristic gives you insight into her favorite things, and you'll find it easier to begin and hold a meaningful conversation with her. It's not just the conversations that you can have with her, though; knowing what

interests Mom can give you an indication of why certain things appeal to her, or why they bring about a reaction in her.

How many times have you asked your mom what she would like as a present for her birthday? Many times, of course, her typical answer was "Just you!" Once you have determined her central characteristic, you will have that vision of the types of things that she likes. The interesting thing is that Mom is probably not even aware that her preferences are so easily identified. Watch her face as you give her something she likes: "How did you know?" is a typical response. Don't try to explain that you knew she liked this or that because her central characteristic says so. Just say that you tried to find something that you "thought she would like." Now when you're out, you may see something you would have overlooked before and say, "I think Mom will like that."

Characteristics of Moms

The following eighteen central characteristics of moms are not meant as a clinical or a psychological description of mothers. We are not clinicians or psychologists; we are people who understand the importance of learning about Mom, and we want to share our knowledge and feelings with you. In the previous section, you read about the benefits of knowing your mom's central characteristic.

Once you have settled on that central characteristic, then you can move on to the next section: "What Your Mom's Central Characteristic Means to You." Be patient. Don't jump ahead to the next section until you have spent the time to truly understand and recognize your mom's central characteristic.

Adventurous

This type of mom does not like to be idle. She wants to be on the go—seeing new places, trying new things, and meeting new people. She will hike up a mountain just to see the view from on top. She will roller-skate in the park for the adrenaline rush. She will not typically be found sitting on the balcony reading a book while on vacation—she is out exploring the town "just to see what's there." This mom also is a risk taker.

Career-Driven

This type of mom is focused on nurturing a long-term working relationship in a given profession or at a particular place of employment. She is totally consumed with her work and is clearly most focused on work-related topics a majority of the time. She will do things that are aimed toward enhancing her position in that profession or at that place of employment. She is willing to make sacrifices now in return for long-term achievements.

Community-Minded

This type of mom is very involved in her local area or anything that affects her neighborhood and community. She might be on the school board, or she may participate in various community activities. She exhibits great concern for her community. This type of mom might hold an elected office in the neighborhood she lives in, and she cares about the little things that make life better for her family. She knows the difference one person can make, and she never takes a back seat when it comes to expressing her opinions and working hard to make her surroundings better.

Controlling

This type of mom needs to be recognized as someone in power and authority. It does not matter if the power is inferential, absolute, or relational—she must be perceived as the one in charge. She will do almost anything to obtain power and keep it. An unfortunate result of her actions can be the demise of relationships. Although, she considers that to be collateral damage, as it is not something that overly concerns her since she prefers things her way.

Difficult

This type of mom is a combination of many other types. She is the one who is not easy to be around for any of a set of reasons.

She might be the type who is headstrong and always right no matter the conversation. Or she could be the egotist who is always correct, even when she is actually wrong. She will give you an excuse to dismiss her error, but she will never admit that she was wrong. This mom just might have a bad attitude all the time that could be the result of a traumatic childhood or a set of unfortunate adult experiences. She is perpetually mad at the world.

Free-Spirited

This mom is truly carefree. She is not concerned with results of actions (or inactions); her focus is on her current activities. She wants to enjoy life, and she wants to live for the moment. This does not mean she takes huge risks. Her attitude is that she will do what she wants to do, and if something happens as a result, so be it. She can be described as "going with the flow."

Helping Others

This type of mom loves to help others and teach them how to help themselves. She gives of herself because it's the right thing to do. This service could be at her children's school, or at a religious institution where she greets people or visits members in the hospital. This mom holds in high regard teaching someone else how to be independent or how to learn a new skill. Giving a cash donation is something your mom will do on occasion, but she really prefers to give her time and talents so that others can "learn to help themselves."

Highly Competitive

This type of mom loves to engage in sports activities where she can play against someone else and, hopefully, win. Competition is her middle name. She may say she plays tennis for the exercise, but she really plays it to beat her opponent and give it that ol' college try. Winning is more important than just playing; it is the primary reason that she does play, and that competitive edge is something she values. Whether it makes her feel young, or in control, or just satisfied that she has won, this type of mom loves winning.

Hobby-Loving

This type of mom loves hobbies where she can relax and feel accomplished. It might be scrapbooking, gardening, or cooking. She finds great relaxation and joy in her hobby of choice. She is happy doing it by herself or with others, just so long as the experience is enjoyable, and not competitive. She likes the solitude these hobbies provide, and the fact that they give her a place where she can think or simply escape the nonstop life she normally lives.

Keeps to Herself

This type of mom is generally quiet. She doesn't say much and is hard to reach and introspective. It appears that she is ignoring you, but don't take that personally. She is "on another wavelength," and you just have to find the right way to get through to her. This type of mom is approachable, but she doesn't give you any indication of how to get her attention. Once you do get her attention, however, she will devote her concentration to you.

Laid-Back

This type of mom might get some things done at home, but at the end of the day, she does not want to do much around the house. She is essentially lazy. The rest of the family must take care of the house, provide the meals, and so on. This mom is content just hanging out in front of the television or reading the newspaper.

Nature-Loving

This type of mom loves being outdoors. She enjoys going for walks on trails as well as uncharted paths. She likes seeing nature as it was meant to be seen, meaning that she would rather have the *chance* to see an animal in the wild than see the same animal in its cage at the zoo. She thinks nature itself is wonderful, and she wants to see it kept that way. She might use a book to keep track of the bird species she has seen, or she just might enjoy watching any bird that comes by.

Scholarly

This type of mom always wants to learn. She views everything she does as a learning experience. When she travels to another country, she takes the time to study the culture and language and visit the museums. She reads about people who have made significant contributions so she might be able to glean something from them. She has high educational aspirations for her children, as do most moms, but academic excellence and educational achievement are of great importance to her. As such, your mom does not take on new encounters lightly—it might take her a while to make a decision, but once she decides, she is committed to her decision.

Self-Absorbed

This type of mom is focused primarily on herself. She might give outward appearances of other characteristics, but her primary activities are centered on herself. This is not a common characteristic, and it is one that generally results from a traumatic or very unpleasant situation. She will not intentionally hurt people or their feelings, but she also is not concerned if she has to "step on people"—or over them—if they are "in her way."

Social Magnet

This type of mom is popular and charismatic in everything she does. Whether she is hosting the party or enjoying a party as an invited guest, people congregate around her, and she naturally attracts others. She is at ease no matter what the function is or who is there. People want to converse with her, be around her, and be seen with her. She can tell jokes, or she can be conversant in the latest news; she seems to be very informed on all the latest happenings. Called "the life of the party," she sees social gatherings as meaningful stimulation and enjoys the company of others.

Success-Driven

This type of mom is focused on being very successful in everything that she does. She might not just focus on a given career; she strives to be successful at everything—at home, at work, and in outside activities. If she takes up a hobby, she will take classes so that she can do her best, and she will spend evenings and weekends perfecting it. Whatever she does, she's going to come out a winner.

Super Mom

This type of mom does it all. She runs a well-organized home and juggles life with loads of balls up in the air. She seems to effortlessly make it all work and still have a great dinner on the table. She always has her family well taken care of. She might get exhausted once in a while and need a break, but she deserves it!

Workaholic

This type of mom must be busy all the time. "Work" or "Chores" is her middle name. Even when she is not at work, she must have several projects that she is working on to keep her happy. She hardly ever sits still. Project-oriented, she generally does not take true "downtime" vacations; she is always working on something, such as taking notes for a future project. She is more focused on being busy than on completion. Completing a project is not critical for her, though it is certainly rewarding. At the same time, this type of mom can completely dismiss one project if another project interests her more.

What Your Mom's Central Characteristic Means to You

You probably had a difficult time deciding on your mom's central characteristic. Most people will find several that appear to fit, and it takes a long time to really decide on the *one* that is truly the characteristic that defines their mom. Good job—you are to be congratulated for persevering through a difficult challenge.

Before we begin, there are a few generalizations that will hold true most of the time. Let's get those out in the open now so we don't have to include them for each characteristic below:

- Ways to begin conversations, and things she would like to discuss: Give your mom some time to relax after she comes home from work or play. You don't have to schedule time, but be respectful of her time and other obligations. Start with, "Mom, when you have a few minutes, I would like to talk with you. Is that okay?" (Of course it's "okay.")

  If you are finding it difficult to get a real conversation started, suggest a safe topic to begin with, and then slowly build on it as you stretch out tangentially from the original discussion.

- Things you can do together: Focus on doing activities that allow the two of you to spend time together—that is not the same as being in the same place and doing the same thing.

Having "Mom radar": Pay attention when she mentions something that is important to her. This might be cleaning out your closet or returning a book to the library so it's not overdue. The key is to be listening and looking out to acknowledge the things that matter to her most. It might be a small item that she will truly enjoy, or it might be just getting her a card to celebrate her latest accomplishment. The more you start really listening to Mom, the more you will learn about Mom and the more Mom will feel like she's special and appreciated.

Her pet peeves, and how to avoid them: Most moms do not like to be disappointed. Do not promise something (to make her happy now) if you don't think you can actually get it done.

Using Mom's Central Characteristic to Learn about Her

Now we will tell you how you can begin a conversation with her (not as straightforward as you might think), offer some ideas on activities that the two of you can do together, give you some suggestions for things to do with Mom that fit her central characteristic, and tell you about some typical pet peeves for moms with that central characteristic.

While we make general observations about each type of mom, your mom has other special qualities. Take the suggestions that we give and then augment them so that they fit your mom.

Adventurous

Being busy in a different way is what makes this type of mom happy. She keeps herself occupied by seeking out new things to do. This is especially true on weekends and on vacations, but she can be adventurous in her work also.

Ways to begin conversations, and things she would like to discuss: Most papers will have a section on exciting adventures. Even if it is only an article, it will cover new and exciting places to go and thrilling things to do. Ask your mom if she read that article, and what she thought of it. If she has been on a recent trip, ask her about it. What was it like? Were there any dangerous moments? Would she do it again? Ask her about the people she has met doing these things. Those people are probably exciting in some way, and hearing about them is certain to be a thrilling time.

Things you can do together: There are many movies of exciting adventures available. Ask your mom if she would like to watch one. She may have seen it already; if so, she might suggest a different one. If it is one she has selected, she will be really interested in it. And if you watch it with her, then you have scored some serious points. In addition to watching a movie, you can suggest a mother–son or a mother–daughter outing. Many adventures are more fun—and certainly safer—if there are two people instead of just one. She will likely be very excited about having you join her. Just remember, she does this because it is exciting—do not expect a leisurely stroll.

Having "Mom radar": What does she like to do? If hiking is her passion, talk to Mom about why she loves this particular activity. Ask her what her favorite and least favorite time hiking was. You could even ask her about her oldest piece of hiking gear—then tell her that you would like to replace it for her. Take her to her favorite store, and let her pick out a new piece of equipment. This private time with her will afford you plenty of time to talk and find out a little more about the things she did when she was your age.

Her pet peeves, and how to avoid them: This mom's top peeve is people who are idle. Relaxing is okay, but she does not like people to just sit around and do nothing. If she asks what you are doing for the weekend, do not reply with "Nothing; probably just watch some TV." A better response would be, "My calendar is flexible right now, Mom. Was there something you wanted to do? I can move things around because I would like to do something with you." If she wants to just drop by, tell her that you would love to see her, but that you are "busy until noon."

Career-Driven

A key point to remember about a career-driven mom is that she focuses on the long-term nature of situations, relationships, and so on. This means that she will not want to hear about any quick fixes or solutions that do not stand the test of time. She will sacrifice for today so she can invest in and for the future.

Ways to begin conversations, and things she would like to discuss: This type of mom is generally straightforward, so the best approach to any conversation is the direct one. Ask her why she decided to get into her profession, and when she made that choice. If she is retired, ask her what was most satisfying about her career. Ask her about current events, and the impact that they have on local and national affairs.

Things you can do together: Just because she is career driven does not mean that she might not like to go to a show with you. Ask her to help you on a project—a school project or one around your house or apartment. If you are still in school, she would probably be willing to talk to your class about her career.

Having "Mom radar": Your radar should easily detect the strong focus that this type of mom has in everything she does, especially toward her job. She likes to stay current in her areas of interest, and these should be very apparent to you.

Your career-driven mom might like a recent book that relates to her work or the chance to attend a seminar on a topic of interest to her. Buy two tickets—one for her and one for you. She will enjoy the seminar, and you will have the chance to spend some valuable time with her (and you might even gain something yourself from the seminar).

If your radar tells you that she loves learning how to do new things, do more than just encourage her. Buy her a how-to book that will help her accomplish something she's wanted to do, like learn to knit or cook. You can put a little note inside the book that she's the greatest mom on earth. If you know a topic of interest to her, buy a subscription to a professional magazine she doesn't have and would enjoy.

Her pet peeves, and how to avoid them: This type of mom doesn't have a lot of time since she has to juggle family and work. Help out with grocery shopping, write down when you run out of household items, or surprise Mom and stock up on things you run out of. Having dinner cooked and on the table when she comes home will be big surprise for her, and it is certain to earn you some "brownie points." Also, be sure to clean up the kitchen mess.

Community-Minded

This type of mom has a great awareness and feeling for her neighbors and friends (who are really the same to her). The community is an important part of her—it defines who she is and so she takes great pride in it. She considers the community to be her home.

Ways to begin conversations, and things she would like to discuss: The local newspaper and local TV news stations are great sources of material for you. There are bound to be several items each day concerning events or happenings affecting the local area. Start by asking your mom's opinion of this thing or that. While it is easy to focus on the negative, she prefers the positive things that are happening. Talk to her about the center for the homeless that just opened or the increase in school funding for elementary education.

Things you can do together: You will make your mom very happy by asking if she would like to attend a local event with you. She might also appreciate your helping her as she rakes the leaves from a neighbor's lawn. Because of her interest in the community, she also cares about how her house looks. If you know that she is going to take on a home improvement project, ask her if she would like some help. She will say yes.

Having "Mom radar": It's a good thing that your radar doesn't have to keep track of this mom, because she spends a lot of her time doing things in and around her community.

This mom has a good heart and cares deeply about improving the community and making it a better place to live for everyone. Think of ways you can assist her with her efforts, like making a donation in her honor. If possible, consider ways to give your time, not just your money, by doing things like volunteering at a nursing home or local school. If she has a fundraiser, purchase a table for you and your friends or contribute something for a silent auction.

The key with this type of mom is to show your support of her efforts by supporting the community cause. She'll be so proud that you took the time, and you'll have something meaningful and purposeful that you share in common.

Her pet peeves, and how to avoid them: This type of mom does not like waste. Don't let her see you wasting time or energy. She also does not like to see litter. She does not like politicians who "talk big," but then do not deliver on their promises. She expects you to back up your words with actions. Don't talk about the time and money that are wasted on community activities. Maybe they are not very efficient, but your mom considers them to be very important activities.

Controlling

This type of mom is the one who is in control of any situation. This is certainly a very natural position for the mother–offspring relationship. You have two choices: Remain in the subservient role or find activities that are neutral and not threatening to her power base.

Ways to begin conversations, and things she would like to discuss: This type of mom is used to having people defer to her. But as her child, you have a special privilege that allows you to start a conversation with a simple, "Mom, I have something I want to discuss with you. Do you have some time?" She will typically say, "Yes," because she relishes the time *with you*. Because of her drive for power, this mom loves "Type A personality" discussions. She will talk about current political hot topics, breaking business news items, and sports (but only the ones she likes).

Things you can do together: You will receive super points if you take your mother to a high-profile event, like a governor's luncheon on a topic that your mom can relate to. She will tell people how she had lunch with the governor, and that you arranged it. (In case you didn't know it, your mom likes to drop names.) Other things you can do together include attending events where she is on a committee, or simply playing a game where one person is declared a clear winner, like Monopoly, chess, or card games.

Having "Mom radar": This type of mom usually does not have a great deal of free time on her hands, but when she does she will read a bestselling book about a powerful person or business. She also enjoys being informed, so when you hear news, keep her posted. When this mom states she's interested in something, that's an excellent clue to the types of things she'd also value discussing with you. Read up on these topics and encourage a better understanding of them by asking your mom questions.

Her pet peeves, and how to avoid them: Because she is such a driver herself, she does not like underachievers. It is hard for her to tolerate those who do not fully apply whatever talents they have. It may seem hard to live up to her standards, but all she really wants for you is to live up to your abilities. Do not criticize people who have made it on their own. You might consider them lucky for one reason or another, but she considers them to be a product of their own hard work. After all, she does not consider herself to be lucky; she has worked for what she has.

Difficult

You will ask yourself many times if it is even worth trying to make any contact with this type of mom. Her combative nature puts up barriers that are difficult to cross. But while the efforts can be huge and largely met with resistance, avoidance, or apathy, don't give up. She is a tougher figure to get through to than any of the other moms we have described, but she is the one who needs it the most. Your ability to relate to her could be the trigger that helps her begin the slow transformation from this central characteristic to another one.

Ways to begin conversations, and things she would like to discuss: There are no standard ways to begin a discussion with this type of mom. Her aggression and volatile nature make it difficult to invade her personal space. One approach is a humble opening like, "Hi, Mom. I've got a couple things I would like to talk with you about. Do you have some time?" This lets her know that you are not in an attacking mode. (She may say she is aggressive because she is used to people attacking her.) Unless there is some bad blood between the two of you, she will probably warm up to you after a light conversation. You will have to let her guide your talks so that she knows that it is safe to talk with you. Once you are able to engage with her for longer conversations, you can start to introduce some new topics, but you will need to exercise restraint and patience.

Things you can do together: You will have to be very open to do almost anything—or do absolutely nothing—to be with your mom. Getting her to talk with you (rather than at you) is a significant first step. Finding things that she wants to do will be a slow process that requires perseverance and a lot of patience. If you know that there are certain things she likes to do, you might suggest one of them. Avoid any "dangerous" activities—ones where your mom is exposed to situations where her bad side comes out.

Having "Mom radar": Even though your mom is very temperamental, it is still important for you to keep your radar turned on. There will be times when she is receptive to talking with you—take advantage of those times! If there is a particular task around the house that she really doesn't like doing, maybe you can do it for her. It not only gives you a chance to be around her, but it also removes a source of her frustration.

Her pet peeves, and how to avoid them: Do not criticize this type of mom, even though it may be justified. Her response will be that she is that way because of something that she can blame on someone or something else.

Free-Spirited

This type of mom is probably the easiest mom to relate to, as long as you are willing to be flexible and adaptive. She is open to so many things that you can just wait for the right moment. She likes spontaneity, which means that you can suggest almost anything to her at the last moment.

Ways to begin conversations, and things she would like to discuss: This mom will talk about almost anything, with an emphasis on "almost." She does not care much for politics, unless the topic impacts the local environment. There are probably many events that interest her, and these make great conversation starters. She will also talk with you about some of her recent activities. If there is anything sitting around that is indicative of something she has done (a souvenir, a photo, and so on), ask her about it and what the activity was like. She will freely talk about it.

Things you can do together: This type of mom will do almost anything with you, even if it is a spur-of-the-moment activity. She likes doing things, and this gives you a lot of freedom for different activities that you can suggest to her that you both do. A simple approach is to just ask her what she would like to do. She will give you an honest answer. If you do not have a lot of time, you can suggest a short walk around the block or even a quick game of cards.

Having "Mom radar": This mom likes a lot of activities, and your radar will be telling you many things. Because of her spontaneity, you have to stay tuned in to know what her current preferences include. If you are willing to do almost anything at the drop of a hat, then be prepared to have a great time with your mom.

She probably has a trip or an outing planned; just ask her what she is doing next. Then ask her if there is something special that you could get for her to make it even more enjoyable. She doesn't always need something tangible, so an alternative would be to pick up the tab for an evening out, be it a play or a movie that you two attend.

Her pet peeves, and how to avoid them: This type of mom does not stick to normal activities, nor does she like to be considered in the majority. She does what she wants, when she wants. Her primary pet peeve is people who do not stray outside the lines. Don't suggest a follow-the-crowd activity or something very structured (such as a guided tour). She also does not plan many things far into the future. She might like the activity once it gets closer, but she doesn't want to commit to it too early.

Helping Others

Seeing someone learn a new skill is a thrill that will never cease to excite this mom. She feels that most people want to be able to do things for themselves. Her service to others is in a teaching mode—helping them to learn to help themselves. This takes many forms, but the constant form is that Mom is there, patiently working with someone until the skill is learned.

Ways to begin conversations, and things she would like to discuss: This mom is happy to talk about the places where she volunteers her time. Beginning a conversation with her can be as simple as, "Mom, tell me a little about the people you help. What is it like? What are the people like?" If you want to see a smile come across her face, ask her to talk about someone whose life has been changed. Once again, she will play down her role. She will say she did just a small part in it—that the greatest contribution came from the person themself. She will tell you about the joy that she sees in these people as they have learned to help themselves.

Things you can do together: While it might seem that working in the same activities as your mom is an automatic choice, this is not necessarily true. Your mom will appreciate your help, but she is more concerned about long-term solutions. This depends, of course, on what the "work" is. Anything you do in the construction of a Habitat for Humanity house will be a tremendous contribution. Another way you two can work together might be to visit garage sales for good books that can be acquired cheaply, and then have her give those books to people who are learning to read.

Having "Mom radar": She is bound to have some personal things she likes, but her priority is others. Consider something that she uses in her work with others. Maybe it is books that she gives to new readers. Maybe she can use a new toolbelt or a hammer for building that Habit for Humanity home. Given that she thinks more of others than herself, she would appreciate donations made in her name. Actually, you don't even have to do it in her name, as she does not need the recognition. Just knowing that you have given to a cause that she likes will make her happy. Does she like to read? Maybe you could find a first edition or an autographed book by one of her favorite authors.

Her pet peeves, and how to avoid them: This type of mom definitely does not like people who have the ability but not the drive. She spends time with people who are trying to improve their lives, and she does not want to be around people who waste opportunities.

Highly Competitive

This type of mom is very active and competitive. She will likely have a fairly strict schedule for her own activities and exercise. This means that you can't just plan on dropping in on her—she is probably busy or away from the house. If you share a common routine like afternoon jogging or walking, you might be able to get some of her time by stopping by in your jogging clothes or walking shoes and suggesting you go for a walk together.

Ways to begin conversations, and things she would like to discuss: Know what your mom is involved in and ask her about these activities. Her competitive spirit makes her inclined to participate in sports, such as tennis, golf, or even racquetball. Ask her about her best game or when she played in the state amateur tournament. This type of mom can also be competitive in other areas such as playing bridge or growing roses.

Things you can do together: What are the things that your mom really likes to do? Pick any one of them and set a date with your mom. If you challenge her to a tennis match, be prepared for the toughest game of your life. Remember, she likes to win, and so she will be playing her hardest. If she is planning to buy a couple more rose bushes for the garden, go with her to the nursery as she picks them out. Ask her why she picked a certain type of rose bush.

Having "Mom radar": Stay on the lookout for what your mom needs to compete. She's an active woman, so her things probably wear out quickly. If your mom is a sports enthusiast, check to see if her sports bag is looking a little tattered. If so, get her a new one. You can even put a new towel inside it. The key is to know what sports she enjoys and then attend her match or support her awards banquet.

Many nurseries will hold gardening classes in the spring. Ask your mom when she has a free weekend, and then sign up for one of these classes. Pay for both of you to attend this class.

Her pet peeves, and how to avoid them: Because she is so active and competitive, she expects others to have an inner drive. She knows this is an unrealistic expectation, but that does not change the fact that she does not like lazy people. Show her that you have a competitive spirit, even if it is not as strong as hers. She wants to see that you have the strong desire to win; make good grades in school or take on challenges in extracurricular activities. Display a sense of determination.

Hobby-Loving

Even though this type of mom likes activities where she can relax, she is still very focused when it comes to work or tasks around the house. Don't mistake her easygoing behavior while gardening or working on a scrapbook for a laid-back attitude. She likes being by herself, but she welcomes your company so long as you respect her desire for a peaceful setting.

Ways to begin conversations, and things she would like to discuss: This mom likes those kinds of activities that can be done alone or in a peaceful environment. Start a conversation by talking about the things that you know she likes. If she likes gardening, ask her which type of tomatoes are the best for cooking. If she likes to make scrapbooks, she will probably have them all over the house. Ask her how she gets her ideas for being so creative in each one.

Things you can do together: There are lots of things to do with this type of mom. Anything that your mom likes to do, you can join her. When you do something with her, though, make sure your attitude and temper are in check. She is there for the enjoyment. Because of her general nature to like peaceful activities, you can suggest many different things that she will do with you.

Having "Mom radar": You have so many possibilities here. An obvious choice is new equipment for her favorite activity. If she likes to work in the garden, you can get a work bucket and put all sorts of items inside it—new gloves, some bulbs for planting, vegetable fertilizer, and so on. Or if she likes tennis, put a container of new tennis balls in her sports bag and tell her that you would like to play a set with her next weekend.

Her pet peeves, and how to avoid them: This type of mom is not a big fan of raucous activities, so don't turn the TV to a boisterous program. When you are out with her playing golf, don't be loud or curse when you make a bad shot. Remember, she likes the peaceful side of sports, and quiet leisure activities.

Keeps to Herself

You might wonder sometimes if this woman is your mom or if she is just someone else who looks like her. She is not the easiest person to get through to, but deep down inside she is still Mom, and she still loves you. Patience on your part is the key to being able to strike up a conversation with her. The wait is worth it because she will focus on you once you have her attention.

Ways to begin conversations, and things she would like to discuss: A simple approach is the best way to open the dialogue; something like, "Hi, Mom. Gee, it's nice to see you." This is a non-threatening opening that does not require her to open up and feel vulnerable. You can begin to move to topics of slightly more substance as she starts to feel more comfortable with the small talk. She will say things that give you openings on topics that she is comfortable discussing. You might have some areas from previous discussions that you know you can talk about, and these can be the safe topics.

Things you can do together: You will find that your mom feels more comfortable in areas that are familiar to her. Her inward nature means that she does not typically like to venture out into new areas, to be in crowded areas, or to participate in activities that require her active involvement. Unless you know some activities to suggest, ask her what she would like to do. While she is a mystery to most people, she will open up to you. Take advantage of the times you have with Mom; they are important to her also, even though she will not openly express those feelings to you.

Having "Mom radar": Your mom will not openly tell you the things that she likes, so you need to keep your radar finely tuned. She is not an open person by nature, but she will talk about certain things in a very general and impersonal manner. You need to have your antennae on at full strength to receive and process this information.

Your mom is not flashy, so anything you get for her must be discreet and subdued. This is the mom who will appreciate a thank-you note, a letter of appreciation from you, or even just some kind words after she has done something.

Her pet peeves, and how to avoid them: You already know that Mom does not like any attention brought to her or to anything she has done. She might be a wealthy philanthropist who does not want any recognition for her charity, or she might be a quiet person who does not want to be in any spotlights. Accept her for who she is. If you want to make a donation on her behalf, make it either as an anonymous donation or in honor of a loved one.

Laid-Back

This type of mom likes forgetting about the day and plopping down in an easy chair. She is a good woman, but she does not want to do much after work. She considers this her right since she provides for her family and is a good mom. It can be a challenge to get close to her because she is not very social. But, you can use this to your advantage because there's less competition for her time and attention.

Ways to begin conversations, and things she would like to discuss: You can ask this mom about television programs because she enjoys most of the primetime shows, and you should already know some of her favorite ones. A simple "What's on tonight, Mom?" will result in a comprehensive listing that compares to the *TV Guide* channel. Given that she does not have many outside interests, finding a mutual conversation topic can be difficult. You will have to rely on your own personal knowledge of things she might like to do or to talk about.

Things you can do together: Watch TV! By nature she is not a very social person, so any activities she does like are generally going to be those in which she does not have to interact with very many people. It is possible that there is an activity that you enjoy—

and she might also—but she has not been exposed to it. It is okay to suggest it, just don't be surprised if she is "not interested."

Having "Mom radar": This type of mom loves being at home, piddling around the house. You can find her watching her favorite shows and just hanging out at home. Keep your radar focused on the shows she really enjoys, and be ready if you know she will be missing one of her favorites. Your laid-back mom will enjoy tapes of her favorite shows when she can't see them, so be sure to catch it on tape.

Did she see the first season of her favorite show? If not, a nice surprise could be getting it on DVD for her. Enclose a little card that says, "I missed the first season too. Maybe we can watch it together?"

Her pet peeves, and how to avoid them: She does not like to be called lazy, even though she may seem that way. If you approach her about it, she will say that she works hard and needs to relax in order to be ready for the next day. She probably has a favorite place to sit—stay away from that seat. She also does not like to be bothered while she is intently watching one of her favorite shows.

Nature-Loving

It is safe to say that this mom has several bird feeders. She loves nature and the things that belong to nature—the trees, the animals, the sounds, and even the quiet of nature. This type of mom would prefer to watch a show on the plains of Africa than the Super Bowl. She feels at peace with nature and considers it natural to go into unspoiled areas.

Ways to begin conversations, and things she would like to discuss: Ask her if she saw the news story on the migrating birds. Make sure you did, because it is possible that she was in the story or contributed to it. If you recently saw a beautiful animal in your yard, tell her about it. She might have a story about it, and tell you what it means ("Cold weather is on its way," for example). If she is the type who will take vacations to go observe nature, ask her about a recent trip. Why did she pick that particular one? What was the best part about it? If you are watching a nature show or movie, ask her to scientifically identify as many species as she can.

Things you can do together: Take a hike! Ask her where she would like to go; even just a nice casual walk through nature can be nice. She has at least a dozen places listed in her brain where she wants to go. She is just looking for an excuse—and a companion—to go. Just being within nature makes her happy.

Having "Mom radar": Pictures are not a top priority with this type of mom. Your radar tells you that she would prefer to see a century flower bloom once than to have a dozen pictures of it. What this means is that if you want to buy something, you will have to be very careful in your selection. Given the things that she likes, you don't have to spend a lot of money.

If the local garden society is sponsoring a nature walk, buy some tickets for her. Go with her and smell the roses. You could even buy tickets in her name and donate them to a nursing home. If she has talked about a certain trip she would like to take "because they won't bloom like this for another ten years," offer to pay for a certain part of the trip. The trip will mean even more because you have recognized it as something that she liked.

Her pet peeves, and how to avoid them: Did you notice the look she gave you when you casually dropped a piece of trash as you were walking? When you carelessly throw something into an area that belongs to nature, you are essentially telling her that her ideals are not worth anything. That hurts her. Respect nature in the same way that you respect people. Remember, she loves you no matter what you do—give her the respect that she deserves.

Scholarly

"What have you learned today?" would be an appropriate motto for this mom. She feels that there is something to be learned in everything you do, and this can be a little bit of a challenge at times. You might want to do something "just for fun," but Mom will turn it into a learning exercise. She expects great things from you academically, but that's because she knows you are capable of outstanding accomplishments.

Ways to begin conversations, and things she would like to discuss: Start by talking about anything educational. This could be something you read in the paper about the local school system or her alma mater. If you are in school, or contemplating going back to school, your mom will love to talk about this; she will probably also have plenty of advice for you.

If she has been on a recent trip, ask her about it. Did she have time to go to any museums? What were her favorite parts of the sights she saw? Ask her to tell you how she incorporates learning into her daily life. She might even have a few suggestions for you.

Things you can do together: She will probably like going to a lecture or discussion about anything that involves learning. The subject is not as important as the setting. If the two of you have similar aptitudes, you might even be able to work together in a mentoring or a tutoring program. The two of you could give a course (some are as short as one night) on something that you both enjoy.

Having "Mom radar": Is there a certain newspaper or magazine that your mom likes? You could get a subscription for her and then sit down and talk with her about it. She will be surprised that you knew, but you don't need to tell her about your radar.

Your radar also probably tells you that she is an avid reader. What genre does she like? Ask your local bookseller for a recommendation, and then get it for her.

This type of mom is probably involved with her alumni association(s). Ask her about her alma mater. Why did she select that school? What did she like about it? If she has thought of attending her college homecoming, tell her you would like to pay for her dinner at the president's table. Watch the look on her face—it will be one of great joy.

Her pet peeves, and how to avoid them: She feels that almost everyone can achieve their goals by continuing to learn. She may feel that you have potential that is not being fully utilized (what parent doesn't?). If you are not planning to further your education (after high school, college, or even a master's), tell her that you are going down a different path right now.

Self-Absorbed

Don't be surprised to discover that this mom does not have many close friends. After all, who wants to be around someone who cares primarily about herself and not others? She might tell you that she has to take care of herself because no one else is watching out for her. This is a defense mechanism that is difficult to overcome; you have to show her that you are not a threat to her.

Ways to begin conversations, and things she would like to discuss: You might have to get permission to talk with this mom. It is not that she does not want to talk with you; rather, she feels the need to have a conversation about her, not with her. The way to start this conversation is to compliment her on something recent. Perhaps her name was in the paper, or you heard of an accomplishment of hers at work—use that as your icebreaker. She will usually take that entrance and begin talking.

She will want to talk about things she has done, a tendency that might make you a little uneasy. As you have more of these conversations with her, you can probably begin to expand the subject matter a little at a time. It will be a slow process, but one that is worth the extra effort.

Things you can do together: Finding good activities is actually easier than talking with this mom. Find out what she likes to do, and then offer to do it with her. Be ready for her penchant to extol her own prowess. If she is giving a talk, attend it and tell her how good it was (she already knows that, but she will like hearing it from you).

Having "Mom radar": Your radar does not have to be very strong to know what this mom likes. She likes almost anything that makes her look good. She may be into status items, such as name-brand clothing or accessories. If you want to get something for her, it will be all that much better if the name is prominently displayed.

This mom has definite opinions about things, so consider where she likes to eat if you're going out to dinner and make sure you're prepared for her feedback. She always wants her opinion to be known.

Her pet peeves, and how to avoid them: Because of her self-centered nature, this mom prefers to have the attention on herself. Chief among her dislikes are public praise for other people and downplaying the importance or value of things she has done. You have to be careful of how you phrase your remarks when she asks a question, especially if it somehow relates to her.

Social Magnet

You will never see a stranger when you are with this type of mom. She knows many people, and she is very likeable. She likes to be around others, and she is stimulated by the buzz of an energetic party. You will be able to see the excitement in her eyes when there is a lot going on—she wants to participate in each discussion because they all interest her.

Ways to begin conversations, and things she would like to discuss: This mom is current on things that matter, whether they are in politics, business, local affairs, health, the social scene, ecology, or even the garden club. Don't start by asking, "Did you see . . . ?" or "Did you hear that . . . ?" Instead, begin the conversation with "Mom, I saw in the news that . . . What do you make of it?" Or, "What do you think of the latest report from . . . ?" If she has recently attended some event, ask her about it. Who was there? What were the highlights?

Things you can do together: This mom is at ease anywhere she goes. The two of you can go for a stroll downtown (careful, though, because she will run into many people she knows). You could visit some art galleries or go to a concert—probably not a rock concert, but you could ask her! She has many other interests, and it should be easy to find something that would fit in with them. It might be a stretch, but the two of you could go to a comedy club for amateur night.

Having "Mom radar": This mom has so many likes that your radar is constantly pinging you with new ideas. She likes to go to new places, such as the opening of an art gallery. She might be busier talking with people than looking at the art. Buy your mom a small item that will remind her of your time together. Write a brief note to give her with the item. Your radar will tell you that she likes things that make her look better. If you get her something, make sure it is the best! She enjoys what's in style and also appreciates entertaining and being part of social events. Use this knowledge to see how you might help her with one of her fundraisers or causes.

Her pet peeves, and how to avoid them: This mom is fairly calm and even-tempered, so she does not have a standard set of pet peeves. But since you know her, you should know what her particular ones are. She might be a neat freak; if so, then don't leave a mess lying around. If she really likes to tell jokes, do not—repeat, do not—spoil her jokes even if you have heard them dozens of times.

Success-Driven

Anything you do with this type of mom must be targeted at her success. This does not mean that you have to lose—a win-win situation will be an optimal one.

Ways to begin conversations, and things she would like to discuss: This type of mom will want to talk about successful people, what they have done to be successful, and what she is doing to be successful. You can talk about what you are doing to further your own success; in fact, she will view your success as a piece of her own.

Things you can do together: You can do almost anything with this type of mom as long as there is some activity involved. She will appreciate going to concerts and museums; she will even go to a lecture with you. This mom wants to be current, which means the two of you can sit and listen to objective and informative newscasts together. Your mom would also enjoy going to one of your alma mater's events. She is proud of what you have accomplished!

Having "Mom radar": This type of mom likes being celebrated and noticed for her efforts. She enjoys doing things well, and she also likes to be appreciated. Keep your radar sharp and be ready to shower Mom with praise when you know she has accomplished something.

Perhaps reward your mom with lunch at a new restaurant near her workplace. Meet the maitre d' and then introduce Mom. She will be very impressed, and it will also show her that her success has been passed down to you. She appreciates good manners. Remember, success takes many forms, and it's important to her that you display what she taught you. Showing that you are successful and well mannered because of the way she raised you will be a reward in itself.

Her pet peeves, and how to avoid them: She does not like failure or when people accept failure as something natural. Do not make excuses if something does not go the right way. Because she is driven, she does not like idle time.

Super Mom

Giving her time, skills, and energy for others' benefit is what defines this mom. She cares about other people, and she is willing to do more than just give a donation.

Ways to begin conversations, and things she would like to discuss: There are bound to be newspaper articles on the various local service organizations your mom worked with. Ask her what it was that gave her the desire to help others. This mom possesses a lot of natural energy; ask her how she keeps her energy level so high, and what suggestions she would have for you.

Things you can do together: Volunteer, volunteer, volunteer! There is always a need for volunteers to work at food banks, homeless shelters, and public television activities; serve food to the homeless; and help to check people in for charity events. Working at one of these places alongside your mom will give you both a great sense of contribution, and the two of you will also have plenty of memories to discuss later.

Having "Mom radar": This is another type of mom that would enjoy a gift given to someone else (nursing homes, crisis centers, elementary schools, or a favorite religious organization). Keep your radar on and figure out Mom's favorite charities, and give a donation to one in honor of her. This contribution has two benefits: the charity benefits, and your mom is proud of you.

Another use for your "Mom radar" is figuring out when she may be feeling overwhelmed and helping her out. Clean the kitchen, water her flowers, or do some laundry to help this Super Mom out.

Her pet peeves, and how to avoid them: This type of mom does not like to hear that people need to be able to take care of themselves. She recognizes that there are many circumstances where people are in unfortunate situations, and they need help. Also, she does not think highly of those who require recognition for their charity work. She thinks people should do good deeds because it is the right thing to do.

Workaholic

It appears that this type of mom is always busy, so you will have to be a little more aggressive to get her time and attention. She will make the time for you, although it might appear that you are interrupting her. Once you have her attention, make good use of the time—she considers it very valuable.

Ways to begin conversations, and things she would like to discuss: Although she will appear to be busy all the time, you can approach her with, "Mom, do you have a few minutes?" She might appear to be ignoring you, but she is actually completing a thought so she can give you her undivided attention. She likes to talk about her projects, so if you show interest in one, she will explain what she is doing and why. When you do have her attention, ask her where she learned her work ethic. No one has probably asked her that before, and that question might allow her to open up a little more to you.

Things you can do together: Given that she is always working, you might ask if she would like some help on a project. Maybe you can help her organize a closet, prepare dinner, or go grocery shopping. She will appreciate the help, and this also gives you the opportunity to have a one-on-one conversation. It is difficult for her to make spur-of-the-moment plans because she is so busy. But if you check a week ahead of time, she might be open to attending an event with you.

Having "Mom radar": This type of mom can always use more time, but there are still only twenty-four hours in a day. One way to spend valuable time with her and to learn more about her is to help her on a project around the house.

Given that she is typically too busy to do much communicating, she will be more open to discussing most things when you two are working together. Use these opportunities to ask her a few questions about her childhood, what her early dreams were, and what her key aspirations are. Along the way you just might pick up some ideas—hints or direct statements on some items that she would like. It might be a new appliance or CD. Give her one of those items with a "just because . . ." card the next time you see her. She will be pleasantly surprised that you knew what she wanted.

Her pet peeves, and how to avoid them: She does not like wasted time, hers or yours. Don't tell her about some project you started and then let lie around. She does not like idle chitchat; conversations, for her, require a meaning. While she might not appear to be extremely organized, in her mind she knows where everything is, and everything she needs to do—do not try to organize her desk or straighten up her study.

Part 2
Questions to Ask Your Mom

Questions to Ask Your Mom

Now that you know so much about Mom—her central characteristic, her likes, her pet peeves—you will be able to approach the following questions with more ease and comfort. You now know why you want to ask these questions and why they are important. It is not that the questions themselves are important. Instead, what matters is that the answers you get from her will add to the reservoir—that body of knowledge—that tells you about Mom. You might think you already know her, but you will be surprised at how much more you learn once you start to talk with her about her childhood, her dreams and goals, and so on.

This is not a notebook to fill out just so it is finished once you have written something on every page. There are no grades, and no one is going to evaluate what you have done (or not done) when you are finished. The only one who will know how well you did is you. What you are doing is gathering information to preserve your mom's legacy today so you will have no regrets tomorrow. We don't know how much time we will have with our moms, so it is imperative that we gather and record as much as we can now—while we can. If this indicates a sense of urgency, then you have gotten the message. Don't wait to talk with Mom—get started immediately!

In case you need a reminder on how to ask the questions, turn to the earlier section "How to Use This Book." There, we gave you some tips on how to start the conversations with Mom; we also gave you three ways to gather the same information if your mom is deceased. That section is a good refresher to read any time that you have set the book down for a while before picking it back up to start asking some questions again. Just like a good tool, this book is valuable only if you use it.

On Mom's Life

"Life is a mystery as deep as ever death can be; Yet oh, how dear it is to us, this life we live and see!"
—Mary Mapes Dodge

The questions in this section offer a glimpse into what Mom remembers as some of the highlights of her childhood and life. Consider this the ideal place to begin a conversation, offering Mom a listening ear and an interested mind. She's a wealth of stories and insights, and the more you learn, the more you'll remember. Plus, Mom will appreciate and enjoy the opportunity to share those special moments from her past and what's especially meaningful to her about her life.

As you and Mom reflect on her childhood, flash back to the time when she was a young girl. Discover what was important to her, what type of child she was, and how she was raised.

Like a puzzle, there will be many aspects of Mom's life that intersect. As she answers each question, try to keep her focused on that specific topic. There will be many questions to ask her that relate to a wide scope of themes as you continue.

Begin by sharing with Mom that these questions are an overview in many ways of her life, how she lived it, and the highlights. Stay centered on each question, asking her to share something specific as you progress. For example, if she starts talking about when she was in the seventh grade, there is probably a story or two that she can tell you. Was there one girl that she always hung around with? Did the two of them tease the boys? Did the same dog bark at them every day on the way home from school?

Pay special attention to her eyes and her facial expressions as she is talking with you about these items that are such an integral part of who she is, and who you are. You will probably see a sparkle in her eyes that you have not seen in a long time. Capture not only the words she is saying, but also the expressions she is using—not just the words but the hand motions, the way she lifts her head to the left and looks into space where all of those dear images are stored. Seal into your own memory bank the calm look on her face; that image could turn out to be one of your dearest memories of her.

Do you know how you got your name? Were you named after a special relative?

_____

_____

_____

_____

_____

_____

_____

_____

_____

_____

_____

_____

_____

Do you know any details about the time when you were born?

_____

_____

_____

_____

_____

_____

_____

_____

_____

_____

_____

_____

_____

_____

Can you share any of the earliest memories of your birthdays?

_____

_____

_____

_____

_____

_____

_____

_____

_____

_____

_____

_____

_____

What are some of your earliest memories about your birthplace and growing up?

_____

_____

_____

_____

_____

_____

_____

_____

_____

_____

_____

_____

_____

If you could go back and visit where you grew up, what is one place you would like to see again? Who is the one person you'd like to see and visit with?

_____

_____

_____

_____

_____

_____

_____

_____

_____

_____

_____

_____

Who were some of your childhood friends, and what special memories do you recall about the times you shared with them?

_____

_____

_____

_____

_____

_____

_____

_____

_____

_____

_____

_____

_____

Do you stay in touch with any of these friends? If so, who are they, and can you tell me how that makes you feel?

_____

_____

_____

_____

_____

_____

_____

_____

_____

_____

_____

_____

_____

How did others describe you when you were a young girl?

_____

_____

_____

_____

_____

_____

_____

_____

_____

_____

_____

_____

_____

_____

Did you have any special chores as a child? What was your least favorite one?

_____

_____

_____

_____

_____

_____

_____

_____

_____

_____

_____

_____

_____

Was there anything you were given as a child that became one of your prized possessions?

_____

_____

_____

_____

_____

_____

_____

_____

_____

_____

_____

_____

_____

Did you play "dress up" as a young girl? Did you play it by yourself, or was it with one of your friends? Who was she?

_____

_____

_____

_____

_____

_____

_____

_____

_____

_____

_____

_____

_____

Do you have any special memories of helping to make dinner when you were growing up? Were there any disasters that you remember?

_____

_____

_____

_____

_____

_____

_____

_____

_____

_____

_____

_____

_____

Where was your favorite place to play as a youngster?

_____

_____

_____

_____

_____

_____

_____

_____

_____

_____

_____

_____

_____

What hobbies did you enjoy during your youth? What hobbies and things do you enjoy most as an adult?

_____

_____

_____

_____

_____

_____

_____

_____

_____

_____

_____

_____

_____

What were you good at as a child? What weren't you good at?

_____

_____

_____

_____

_____

_____

_____

_____

_____

_____

_____

_____

_____

What accomplishment in your life are you proudest of?

_____

_____

_____

_____

_____

_____

_____

_____

_____

_____

_____

_____

_____

Is there anything you have done in your life that you regret?

_____

_____

_____

_____

_____

_____

_____

_____

_____

_____

_____

_____

_____

On Our
Family History

"Let your children blossom as if they are beautiful flowers in nature. They will need a strong foundation and room to grow."

—RFS

Mom's family history helped shape her into the woman she is today. The following questions are very important, for they pay a loving tribute to her life, including her parents and family. Mom's family history also impacts your life and your children's lives, so pay attention to the little details that you learn along the way.

This section contains questions you can ask your mom about her family and the things they did when she was younger. This also gives you a chance to gain a better understanding of why she is the way she is. You might not like everything you hear or read, but all of it is a part of what makes you who you are.

When you hear or read something about your family history that you did not already know, try asking a probing question to learn even more about it—to get beyond the superficial answer. For example, if your mom says that her family's favorite vacation spot when she was young was the lake house with a pier that jutted out into the water, you might try to find out why. Was it close to the house, or was it far away? Did they go there because the family owned the house, or were there other reasons why they chose that?

When you start to write down the information you want to pass along to *your* children, this section on your mom's family history will be very important. This is where your children will find out about their grandma as well as other relatives who were rarely seen. This section can really be fun because you are able to learn so much more about other members of the family tree—those aunts and uncles, and maybe even your grandparents, whom you saw occasionally but did not spend a lot of time with.

Depending on the family dynamics in your mom's life, this section might be a little touchy. If this is the case, we suggest that you save this section until after you have already talked with your mom on several other sections. By starting in some of the easier sections, you will be able to establish a rapport that becomes more conversational rather than just an interviewing situation. Once you have developed that kind of bond that allows you to ask almost anything, then you can come back to this section.

Is there anything you wish you could have asked your mom but never got around to?

_____

_____

_____

_____

_____

_____

_____

_____

_____

_____

_____

_____

_____

What would you like future generations to know about your parents?

_____

_____

_____

_____

_____

_____

_____

_____

_____

_____

_____

_____

_____

What would you like future generations to know about your grandparents and our family history?

_____

_____

_____

_____

_____

_____

_____

_____

_____

_____

_____

_____

_____

What was the best advice your mom gave you when you were younger that has always stayed on your mind?

_____

_____

_____

_____

_____

_____

_____

_____

_____

_____

_____

_____

_____

What was the best advice your dad gave you when you were younger that has always stayed on your mind?

_____

_____

_____

_____

_____

_____

_____

_____

_____

_____

_____

_____

_____

_____

Can you share what you loved most about your mother?

_____

_____

_____

_____

_____

_____

_____

_____

_____

_____

_____

_____

_____

Can you share one story about her that you would want passed on to the next generation?

_____

_____

_____

_____

_____

_____

_____

_____

_____

_____

_____

_____

_____

Can you share what you loved most about your father? What is one special memory of him that makes you feel special as his daughter?

_____

_____

_____

_____

_____

_____

_____

_____

_____

_____

_____

_____

Can you share any special traditions, gatherings, or family get-togethers that you particularly remember?

_____

_____

_____

_____

_____

_____

_____

_____

_____

_____

_____

_____

_____

What traditions that are important to you do you wish we'd continue, and why?

_____

_____

_____

_____

_____

_____

_____

_____

_____

_____

_____

_____

_____

What traditions did you share with your extended family?

_____

_____

_____

_____

_____

_____

_____

_____

_____

_____

_____

_____

_____

How did you get along with your brothers and sisters? If you are an only child, were there special friends who seemed like a brother or a sister to you? What special stories do you remember about them?

_____

_____

_____

_____

_____

_____

_____

_____

_____

_____

_____

_____

What family member did you most look up to and want to be like?

_____

_____

_____

_____

_____

_____

_____

_____

_____

_____

_____

_____

_____

What family member was the most interesting? Why did he or she fascinate you?

_____

_____

_____

_____

_____

_____

_____

_____

_____

_____

_____

_____

_____

Do you have a favorite family photograph that you could show me and tell me all about? Why is that photograph special to you?

_____

_____

_____

_____

_____

_____

_____

_____

_____

_____

_____

_____

_____

What do you think made our family special and that you hope is carried on by the next generation?

_____

_____

_____

_____

_____

_____

_____

_____

_____

_____

_____

_____

_____

On Mom's Values

"He used to say that it was better to have one friend of great value than many friends who were good for nothing."

—Diogenes Laertius

This section focuses on Mom's values. These are the beliefs your mom lives her life by and that challenge you as well to be the best person you can be. Values inspire us to do the right thing, and when we do, we honor the core values that a good life is based on. As you ask Mom about the principles that she cares most about, consider your own values. Did you learn them from Mom? Did she encourage you to live your life by these guiding thoughts and ideals? Are you following along the path that you know you should?

It's not easy to do, but an honest, open reflection on your mom's beliefs might help you face times that require some serious soul-searching.

Many people automatically connect having values to being religious. There certainly can be a connection there, but **everyone** can have values in their life, and we know that not everyone is religious. Our values are the core of what and who we are. Have you ever been in a situation where you could have gotten away with something, but you chose the honorable way? Why did you make the right choice? Were you afraid that someone might see you, and you would then feel guilty? Or did you do the right thing just because it was the right thing to do? Did you learn your values from Mom?

Most of us are products of our environments, and it would be very natural for your values to mirror your mom's. After you have the answers to these questions about Mom, think about how you would answer the same questions. Are the answers the same? Are they at least similar? What do you think could be the reason if the answers are vastly different?

A valid question that you might want to ask us is this: "But what if my mom's values are **not** the ones that I really want to mirror?" We do not want to do any preaching in this book about moral judgments or what is right and what is wrong. You're a grownup, and you can make those choices for yourself.

What one or two things would you want me to be certain of, to know, or to understand as I go through life?

_____

_____

_____

_____

_____

_____

_____

_____

_____

_____

_____

_____

_____

Are you afraid of dying? What is it that you fear most? What will you miss the most?

_____

_____

_____

_____

_____

_____

_____

_____

_____

_____

_____

_____

_____

Has your faith ever been tested? How did you handle it? What advice do you have for me?

_____

_____

_____

_____

_____

_____

_____

_____

_____

_____

_____

_____

_____

How do you handle life when things feel overwhelming?

How do you handle disappointment? What example can you give me so that I can be better prepared when I have to face it?

_____

_____

_____

_____

_____

_____

_____

_____

_____

_____

_____

_____

_____

_____

Can you share your memories of a time when you spoke up for someone?

_____

_____

_____

_____

_____

_____

_____

_____

_____

_____

_____

_____

_____

Can you share a motto you have lived your life by, or a good deed you have performed that gave you the greatest satisfaction? What was your inspiration at the time?

_____

_____

_____

_____

_____

_____

_____

_____

_____

_____

_____

_____

_____

What do you value most when it comes to friends, and what kind of a friend are you to others?

_____

_____

_____

_____

_____

_____

_____

_____

_____

_____

_____

_____

_____

Who are your friends—the ones you can count on to be there no matter what?

_____

_____

_____

_____

_____

_____

_____

_____

_____

_____

_____

_____

_____

If you could change one thing about yourself, what would it be?
Why would you want to make that change?

_____

_____

_____

_____

_____

_____

_____

_____

_____

_____

_____

_____

_____

What moral dilemmas have you faced? What did you rely upon to get through them?

_____

_____

_____

_____

_____

_____

_____

_____

_____

_____

_____

_____

_____

What has been your basis for handling peer pressure—both as a youth and as an adult?

_____

_____

_____

_____

_____

_____

_____

_____

_____

_____

_____

_____

_____

_____

On Marriage and Relationships

"One should believe in marriage as in the immortality of the soul."
—Honoré de Balzac

The topic of love, marriage, and relationships is certainly an important one. Approach these questions with care. Some moms are willing to address these topics freely, while others are more reserved about addressing their relationships. Depending on the nature of your family structure, you might consider including your dad in these discussions, if that is possible.

Consider what's important in this section for you to accomplish. What do you really want to know? What might help you later in life as you deal with relationship issues or otherwise? Perhaps you want to better understand Mom's feelings, and these questions will give you a glance into her heart and what matters most to her.

We know that some people have parents who are divorced or separated for various reasons. That does not mean that you should not ask these questions. You may have to approach Mom in a slightly different manner, but it is still very important to know her feelings. After you and she have worked through several of the "easier" sections, you could say something like this: "Mom, we are now coming to some questions that might seem a bit awkward given the circumstances. But I know you must have cared a lot about Dad when you married him. Those are the feelings I want to know about. Those are the memories that I hope you can share with me."

You are asking her to address some issues that are probably difficult for her, especially if she is on the stubborn side. Don't press her if she is not ready to answer these questions right now.

In addition to marriage, does your mom have other relationships that have been formed over the years? Are there people from work, or around the neighborhood, with whom she seems to enjoy spending time? Does she like to visit certain people when she travels? As you find out more about these other people in your mom's life, you will learn more about how she values relationships. You will also gain more insight into the reasons that your family is the way it is.

What were your hopes and dreams for your children when it comes to marriage? What advice do you think I should give my children before they get married?

_____

_____

_____

_____

_____

_____

_____

_____

_____

_____

_____

_____

_____

How did you first meet Dad? What were your first thoughts? Was it love at first sight?

_____

_____

_____

_____

_____

_____

_____

_____

_____

_____

_____

_____

_____

What can you share about your first date with Dad?

_____

_____

_____

_____

_____

_____

_____

_____

_____

_____

_____

_____

_____

What is it about Dad that makes you love him so much?

_____

_____

_____

_____

_____

_____

_____

_____

_____

_____

_____

_____

_____

How have you and Dad learned to deal with your differences?

_____

_____

_____

_____

_____

_____

_____

_____

_____

_____

_____

_____

_____

When did you know that you wanted to marry Dad? How did he propose to you?

_____

_____

_____

_____

_____

_____

_____

_____

_____

_____

_____

_____

_____

Have you ever doubted your marriage? What was it that caused you to have doubts?

_____

_____

_____

_____

_____

_____

_____

_____

_____

_____

_____

_____

_____

[If your mom has been married more than once] How come your first marriage did not work out? When did you first feel that it was in trouble?

_____

_____

_____

_____

_____

_____

_____

_____

_____

_____

_____

_____

What do you wish you knew then that you know now about relationships, in life and in love?

_____

_____

_____

_____

_____

_____

_____

_____

_____

_____

_____

_____

_____

Who are some of the people in your life that you consider your best friends? What makes your relationships so special?

_____

_____

_____

_____

_____

_____

_____

_____

_____

_____

_____

_____

_____

On Mom's Dreams and Goals

"A goal is a dream with a deadline."
—Harvey Mackay

All moms hope for the future to be bright, happy, and prosperous, especially when it comes to providing for their families. The future of your mom's loved ones is her waking concern—that those things she has worked for and hoped for will become a reality. Search for the lessons she learned along the way, and encourage a conversation that will offer you insight into how your mom overcame adversity, rose to the occasion during difficult times, and not only obtained success, but also accomplished what she had always hoped for.

As she is answering these questions, try to dig deeper for more information. How was she feeling at the time? Did she know for certain what her path in life would be? Who was giving her the encouragement she needed? These follow-up questions will give you additional insight that you can use when you are addressing similar situations. Share with Mom your own hopes and dreams, for you will discover that your success is ultimately her greatest accomplishment as well. She might even be willing to offer you some guidance on how she would have handled the situations you are facing.

Your mom's generation was brought up with different goals than most of us have today. They had come through hard times (depressions, wars, recession), so it is not unusual if some of their goals might seem simple to you. Do not discount the fact that a primary motivator in your mom's life might have been to see you go to college, or for her to be able to retire to a comfortable life. What might seem like a given to you could have been a stretch for your mom. Let her know how much you appreciate the sacrifices she made so that you could have an easier life.

Once again, if there is any one section where you do not want to be judgmental, this is it. If your mom's dreams and goals sound mundane to you, try to put yourself in her position when she was your age—did she have any luxuries that you now consider necessities? Was she living at home while going to school, or was she working two jobs? If you want to feel humble, put yourself in your mom's shoes and see how well you would do in the same situation.

What did you want to be when you were a little girl?

_____

_____

_____

_____

_____

_____

_____

_____

_____

_____

_____

_____

When you were older, was there any particular job or career that you envisioned yourself doing when you grew up? What attracted you to that?

_____

_____

_____

_____

_____

_____

_____

_____

_____

_____

_____

_____

_____

What is your greatest accomplishment in life? What would have been your answer ten years ago? Twenty years ago?

_____

_____

_____

_____

_____

_____

_____

_____

_____

_____

_____

_____

_____

What is one dream you have not made come true yet, but you hope one day to make happen?

_____

_____

_____

_____

_____

_____

_____

_____

_____

_____

_____

_____

_____

If you ever wrote a book, what would it be about?

_____

_____

_____

_____

_____

_____

_____

_____

_____

_____

_____

_____

_____

Can you share a time that you were disappointed because one of your goals or dreams did not come true, but you rose above it?

_____

_____

_____

_____

_____

_____

_____

_____

_____

_____

_____

_____

How did you go about resetting your goal or your dream?

_____

_____

_____

_____

_____

_____

_____

_____

_____

_____

_____

_____

_____

Do you have any regrets in life, things that you wish you had done differently? Is it too late to do them now?

_____

_____

_____

_____

_____

_____

_____

_____

_____

_____

_____

_____

_____

What goals do you think you might have if you were my age today? How different are they from the goals you had when you were my age? What makes them different?

_____

_____

_____

_____

_____

_____

_____

_____

_____

_____

_____

_____

What has been your main source of motivation? When did that start?

_____

_____

_____

_____

_____

_____

_____

_____

_____

_____

_____

_____

_____

Do you listen to, or have you listened to, motivational tapes or CDs? How do they inspire you? How long does that burst of inspiration last?

_____

_____

_____

_____

_____

_____

_____

_____

_____

_____

_____

_____

_____

Do you keep a written list of your goals? What do you do to keep them fresh in your mind?

_____

_____

_____

_____

_____

_____

_____

_____

_____

_____

_____

_____

What book or books would you recommend that I read one day?

_____

_____

_____

_____

_____

_____

_____

_____

_____

_____

_____

_____

_____

Do you have a favorite movie that inspired you?

_____

_____

_____

_____

_____

_____

_____

_____

_____

_____

_____

_____

On Parenting
and Children

"These are thy glorious works,
Parent of good!"

—John Milton

Being a mother is a full-time job. From supporting a family to raising children, a mother's responsibilities are often the core of her existence. This selection of questions focuses on the type of mom your mother is or was. It's a wonderful opportunity to let Mom know what she did that helped you grow up into the person you are today. This is not to take anything at all away from everything that your dad did—both of them worked hard to give you the life that you had.

Once you become a parent, you also appreciate your own parents more than ever. It's a huge job and one of the most rewarding ones in life. The questions in this section will help you learn a great deal about your parents' joy when you were born. Here are the little details that fade over time, from the day you were born to how your mother and/or father selected your name. This is an especially wonderful chapter since it's your heritage that Mom will address.

As your mom talks about you when you were very young, she might get a little off-track in her conversation—allow her that freedom. In fact, you can probably use this side conversation to find out even more about her. If she mentions anything about the house where you lived back then, ask about the neighbors. Were they close friends? Did the families do things together? Even if there are not specific questions in this book along these lines, this allows your mom more freedom to talk about her wonderful memories.

If you are already a parent, then this chapter will have an extra special meaning. Ask your mom questions that will help you be the best parent you can be. Think about your own parenting style— what have you learned from your mother that you are passing down to your children? Use this section as a catalyst to gain clarity about what matters most to you, and then consider how it affects your own children. If you see some characteristics in your mom as a parent that you do not want to pass on to your children, keep that to yourself. This is another area where it might be easy to judge your mom (and your dad) on the way you were brought up—please don't. See what lessons you can take from those experiences, and make the necessary adjustments in your own role as a parent.

How did you and Dad decide on my name and its spelling? Did you use books to look up names, or did you want to use a name that was special to you? How far in advance did you agree on my name?

_____

_____

_____

_____

_____

_____

_____

_____

_____

_____

_____

_____

_____

Can you share any details about the day I was born? What was the weather like? Was there a lot of traffic as you drove to the hospital?

_____

_____

_____

_____

_____

_____

_____

_____

_____

_____

_____

_____

_____

How did life change for you when I was born?

_____

_____

_____

_____

_____

_____

_____

_____

_____

_____

_____

_____

_____

Can you think of a time when I was a baby that we did something special together?

_____

_____

_____

_____

_____

_____

_____

_____

_____

_____

_____

_____

_____

What did I do that drove you crazy when I was a toddler?

_____

_____

_____

_____

_____

_____

_____

_____

_____

_____

_____

_____

_____

What is one thing I have done that has made you proud of me?

_____

_____

_____

_____

_____

_____

_____

_____

_____

_____

_____

_____

How do you manage to unconditionally love your children, no matter what?

_____

_____

_____

_____

_____

_____

_____

_____

_____

_____

_____

_____

_____

What weren't you great at when I was little?

_____

_____

_____

_____

_____

_____

_____

_____

_____

_____

_____

_____

What did you teach me to do when I was younger that you were proud of?

_____

_____

_____

_____

_____

_____

_____

_____

_____

_____

_____

_____

_____

What activities did you love to share with me? Was there a favorite time that you recall was memorable?

_____

_____

_____

_____

_____

_____

_____

_____

_____

_____

_____

_____

If you were to give me one piece of advice based on what you have learned as a mother that I should know and pass down to my children, what would it be?

_____

_____

_____

_____

_____

_____

_____

_____

_____

_____

_____

_____

_____

Do you think it was harder to raise children when I was young than it is today?

_____

_____

_____

_____

_____

_____

_____

_____

_____

_____

_____

_____

_____

What were some of the things you had to do then that are taken for granted today when raising a child?

_____

_____

_____

_____

_____

_____

_____

_____

_____

_____

_____

_____

_____

How did you maintain sanity when you had noisy kids running around the house all day long?

_____

_____

_____

_____

_____

_____

_____

_____

_____

_____

_____

_____

_____

Would you have wished for more children? Why? Why didn't you have more?

_____

_____

_____

_____

_____

_____

_____

_____

_____

_____

_____

_____

_____

How did we behave as children compared to the neighbors' children?

_____

_____

_____

_____

_____

_____

_____

_____

_____

_____

_____

_____

_____

On Mom's Legacy

"The legacy we leave is not just in our possessions, but in the quality of our lives."

—Billy Graham

This section contains questions you can ask your mom about the things she wants people to remember about her. When you think about your mom, it is important to know her thoughts, her feelings, her likes, her dislikes—all the things that make her unique and that she wants people to hold on to and not forget. None of us lives forever, but that does not mean that this section has to focus on our mortality. As you are asking these questions, try to focus on the things that are truly "Mom." As you look at a question, go beyond the simple one- or two-sentence answer. Expand on the answer with an example of something your mom did that made it very memorable—for her or for you. If your mom wanted to be known for being able to whip up a dinner on a moment's notice, take it an extra step and find out if there were ever any times when the recipe didn't turn out exactly as planned. Or perhaps she was just about done, and the power went out and she could not finish cooking. Try to find that extra dimension in the answers that is not always offered right away. Those are the stories that are fun to pass along.

Keep these thoughts in mind as you are talking with your mom about this section. You may have other thoughts, and that's okay. We just want to offer these as a guiding path in case you need one.

- Throughout your life, your mom's love has brightened your world. A life without her physical presence might seem unbearable and impossible, but sadly, one day, that will become a reality.
- This section is devoted to helping Mom craft the future—from what she wants you to remember, to her words that she hopes you'll hear.
- Honor her life by celebrating what she cared about and believing in and more.
- Let Mom's legacy be based on love, and instill in your heart her words of wisdom and insights into her life.
- This is the time to make sure that you have everything you need to preserve her legacy today so you have no regrets tomorrow.

What is the one main thing you would want to say to your family before you die?

_____

_____

_____

_____

_____

_____

_____

_____

_____

_____

_____

_____

_____

How do you want to be remembered?

_____

_____

_____

_____

_____

_____

_____

_____

_____

_____

_____

_____

_____

What specific things do you want us to do when you pass away?

_____

_____

_____

_____

_____

_____

_____

_____

_____

_____

_____

_____

_____

If you were to describe the perfect funeral, what would it look like? Who would you want to give your eulogy? What would you want them to say?

_____

_____

_____

_____

_____

_____

_____

_____

_____

_____

_____

_____

_____

_____

One day, when I am describing you to future generations, what would you want me to share about you?

_____

_____

_____

_____

_____

_____

_____

_____

_____

_____

_____

_____

_____

_____

What possessions would you want us to keep and pass down?
Why are those things important to you?

_____

_____

_____

_____

_____

_____

_____

_____

_____

_____

_____

_____

_____

What pictures of you should I hold most dear? What memories do they bring to you?

_____

_____

_____

_____

_____

_____

_____

_____

_____

_____

_____

_____

What are some key words that you want me to always remember?
What special thoughts and feelings do they evoke for you?

_____

_____

_____

_____

_____

_____

_____

_____

_____

_____

_____

_____

Who Knows Mom Best?

This section is especially important if you want to learn about your mom through the eyes of others. It is very helpful if your mom is modest, won't say much, or perhaps is even deceased. Consider the amount of time your mom has spent with friends, other family members, neighbors, and coworkers. This is your chance to ask these people about their favorite memories of your mom, and their feelings about her, and to preserve those memories that perhaps would be long forgotten.

If your mom is no longer with you, then you will actually be doing a favor for those whom you contact. They will feel special because you have taken the time to ask them about your mom. There will be some tears shed as they tell you why she was so special. Think of those tears, and the ones you shed, as being the glue that ties all those special memories together.

There are two sets of the "Who Knows Mom Best?" questions, but you can photocopy these pages to ask more than two people the questions.

Who Knows Mom Best?

What did you think of my mom the first time you met her?

_____

_____

_____

_____

What are some of the most special memories you have of her?

_____

_____

_____

_____

If you had to sum up my mom in one word, what would that be?
Why did you choose that particular word?

_____

_____

_____

_____

Is there anything my mom taught you that inspired you and that you recall to this day?

_____

_____

_____

_____

Was there a time when my mom helped you in any way?

_____

_____

_____

_____

At that time, how well did you know her, and how did it change your relationship?

_____

_____

_____

_____

What do you think was most important to my mom?

_____

_____

_____

_____

What do you think my mom did best?

_____

_____

_____

_____

What were her strengths?

_____

_____

_____

_____

What were some of my mom's weaknesses?

_____

_____

_____

_____

Was there a time when my mom was stubborn?

_____

_____

_____

_____

If you were to describe your favorite things about my mom, what would they be?

_____

_____

_____

_____

Is there any other special memory you have of my mom?

_____

_____

_____

_____

Who Knows Mom Best?
What did you think of my mom the first time you met her?

_____

_____

_____

_____

What are some of the most special memories you have of her?

_____

_____

_____

_____

If you had to sum up my mom in one word, what would that be?
Why did you choose that particular word?

_____

_____

_____

_____

Is there anything my mom taught you that inspired you and that you recall to this day?

_____

_____

_____

_____

Was there a time when my mom helped you in any way?

_____

_____

_____

_____

At that time, how well did you know her and how did it change your relationship?

_____

_____

_____

_____

What do you think was most important to my mom?

_____

_____

_____

_____

What do you think my mom did best?

_____

_____

_____

_____

What were her strengths?

_____

_____

_____

_____

What were some of my mom's weaknesses?

_____

_____

_____

_____

Was there a time when my mom was stubborn?

_____

_____

_____

_____

If you were to describe your favorite things about my mom, what would they be?

_____

_____

_____

_____

Is there any other special memory you have of my mom?

_____

_____

_____

_____

Mom's Favorite Things

From Mom's favorite foods to movies to places to travel, this section is a special reminder of Mom's favorite pastimes. Exploring each one of these areas will be like opening up a treasure chest. Your mom will certainly have a story or two to tell—if you ask for more information—about each of these. For example, don't just stop once she tells you the name of her favorite restaurant. Ask her more: Why does she like it so much? Was there one time that was more special than any other? Is that restaurant where she likes to go for very special occasions? Do the waiters know her by name? You can do a similar type of additional exploration for each of the questions. Have fun exploring!

If your mom is no longer with you, you can still fill out this section by asking other family members and friends. They will be happy to help you on your journey—asking them will also help them remember your mom one more time. That will be a treat for them.

Leisure Time

Favorite hobbies:

_____

_____

_____

_____

_____

_____

_____

_____

_____

_____

_____

_____

_____

_____

Favorite holiday:

_____

_____

_____

_____

_____

_____

_____

_____

_____

_____

_____

_____

_____

Favorite ways to pass the time:

_____

_____

_____

_____

_____

_____

_____

_____

_____

_____

_____

_____

Good Eats

Favorite foods for breakfast:

_____

_____

_____

_____

_____

_____

Favorite foods for lunch:

_____

_____

_____

_____

_____

_____

Favorite foods for dinner:

_____

_____

_____

_____

_____

_____

Favorite meals to make:

_____

_____

_____

_____

_____

_____

Least favorite food:

_____

_____

_____

_____

_____

_____

Favorite restaurant:

_____

_____

_____

_____

_____

_____

People, Places, and Entertainment
Person(s) you most admire:

_____

_____

_____

_____

_____

_____

_____

_____

_____

_____

_____

_____

_____

_____

Best advice you were ever given:

_____

_____

_____

_____

_____

_____

_____

_____

_____

_____

_____

_____

_____

Favorite place(s) for a vacation:

_____

_____

_____

_____

_____

_____

_____

_____

_____

_____

_____

_____

_____

_____

Favorite movies:

_____

_____

_____

_____

_____

_____

Favorite movie stars:

_____

_____

_____

_____

_____

_____

Favorite television shows when you were younger:

_____

_____

_____

_____

_____

_____

Favorite television show now:

_____

_____

_____

_____

_____

_____

Around the World with Mom
Places Mom has visited:

_____

_____

_____

_____

_____

_____

_____

_____

_____

_____

_____

_____

_____

_____

Friends Mom made while traveling:

_____

_____

_____

_____

_____

_____

_____

_____

_____

_____

_____

_____

Memories from Mom's favorite cities:

_____

_____

_____

_____

_____

_____

_____

_____

_____

_____

_____

_____

_____

Memories from Mom's favorite cities:

_____

_____

_____

_____

_____

_____

_____

_____

_____

_____

_____

_____

_____

_____

Trips that were extra-special:

_____

_____

_____

_____

_____

_____

_____

_____

_____

_____

_____

_____

_____

_____

Trips that were extra-special:

_____

_____

_____

_____

_____

_____

_____

_____

_____

_____

_____

_____

_____

_____

A Few Final Words

We hope that you have found this book to be very helpful. We know that not every relationship between a child (of any age) and his or her mom is the ideal relationship, but there is a special bond that will always exist between them. Whether you used this book to learn more about your mom or you are the mom passing on information to your children, the thoughts and discussions you had alone or with others will also become a significant part of the shared memories. If this book has helped you to have more family discussions, please leverage that and have more family discussions—even the casual ones will have a more special meaning to all of you.

Make the most of it. Before the day ends, tell someone in your family, "I love you," and continue to share the words that were lovingly recorded in the pages of this very special book. Keep in mind that time is a memory that we must store in our hearts. We feel certain that Mom would like that.

Stuart Gustafson is an author, mathematician, engineer, and college instructor who has recently retired from the corporate world. He has a BA in Mathematics from San Diego State University and an MBA from the University of San Diego. In addition to writing, Stuart enjoys traveling and spending time with his family. He is married to Darlene Smith, and they have a daughter Adrianne and a son Woodrow. Stuart and Darlene live in Boise, Idaho. Visit *www.stuartgustafson.com* for more information.

Robyn Freedman Spizman is an award-winning author who has written dozens of inspirational and educational nonfiction books during her career, including *Make It Memorable*, *When Words Matter Most*, *GIFTionary*, and *The Thank You Book*. She also coauthored the Women for Hire series (with Tory Johnson) and debuted her first novel for young readers, Secret Agent (with Mark Johnston). As a seasoned media personality and consumer advocate for more than twenty-four years, she has appeared often on NBC's *Today* and CNN and is featured regularly on the NBC Atlanta affiliate WXIA and Star 94. She lives in Atlanta with her husband and is the proud mother of two grown children, Justin and Ali. Visit *www.robynspizman.com* for more information.